BLUFF

TAX

A.J. CARROLL

ℛ
RAVETTE PUBLISHING

Published by Ravette Publishing Limited
P.O. Box 296
Horsham
West Sussex RH13 8FH

Telephone: (01403) 711443
Fax: (01403) 711554

Series Editor – Anne Tauté

Cover design – Jim Wire, Quantum
Printing & binding – Cox & Wyman Ltd.
Production – Oval Projects Ltd.

The Bluffer's Guides™ series is based
on an original idea by Peter Wolfe.

The Bluffer's Guides™, Bluffer's™
and Bluff Your Way™ are Trademarks.

An Oval Project
for Ravette Publishing.

CONTENTS

INTRODUCTION

Tax is a game. Like most other games it is played between two teams, in this case The Taxman v the Rest of the World.

It has both written and unwritten rules, which have to be learnt by both sides. There are referees, such as the Parliamentary Ombudsman and the European Court of Justice. Some games are quiet local matches with no-one turning out except the players. Others are televised and reported worldwide. Players can be off-side or sent off, like Lester Piggott, Nissan UK and Steffi Graff's Dad.

The pitch markings for the game are unclear, so neither side knows how to behave in the grey areas around the edges. This makes it more interesting for good players.

Tax is also played on many levels, like a computer game, so experts can travel through income tax and personal allowances to the highest levels of international tax. But one wrong move may mean relegation to a lower division.

Unwillingly and unwittingly, you too are a player in this game. This guide will help you to keep control, rather than trip over the ball. It may also help you understand what happens to the money you give away every day to people you have never met.

THE BASICS

Most governments regard people as sheep, who are fleeced regularly by taxes. The aim is: maximum wool, minimum bleating. If you become an effective tax bluffer, you are less likely to have this wool pulled over your eyes. The first step is to grasp the basics: what is taxed, why, and how.

What

Food, drink, income, capital, petrol, pensions, dying, betting, telephones and rubbish are all taxed, but this complexity can be reduced to a few basic principles. Tax is really only charged on three things:

Bodies, whether dead or alive, as in Death Duties or Poll Tax.

Assets, including money, land and houses.

Transactions, such as buying and selling.

This abbreviates as **BAT**, and helps to explain the widespread fear of flying mammals. Tax systems really suck your blood.

Why

The truth is, a great deal of taxpayers' money has always been frittered away on ill-designed projects or amusements. But because it is dangerous and insensitive for rulers to admit this, they have always bluffed.

In the old days, taxes were to pay for war, to keep the peace or to protect the people from Saladin or the

Tzar of Russia. Today, their bluff is more sophisticated. Tax is a necessary good, providing funding for a whole range of social benefits. It also has a secondary use, as a psychological weapon, a form of aversion therapy. Governments impose heavy taxes on some behaviour, such as smoking and drinking, but reward desirable actions – like getting married – with tax relief.

What is encouraged or discouraged changes over time. In the 1930s, the German fiscal system supported people with children; conversely, if a Chinese couple break the 'one child' policy, two years' earnings may be taken in tax.

How

All taxes are either **direct** or **indirect**. Direct tax hits you between the eyes. Income tax and capital gains tax are direct taxes. Indirect tax is like living on a plateau: you tend to forget you are not at sea level. Without realising it, you pay a base level of indirect taxes as part of everyday costs.

Occasionally indirect taxes *are* noticeable, like mountain peaks rising from the plains. This is when the cost increase is particularly high, such as duties on tobacco, perfume, and alcohol. Even then the peak is only really noticeable when you go abroad, and realise how cheap the wine is.

THE FAMOUS FIVE

Most tax systems have five main characters, without whom it is difficult to write a script at all. There are also a host of minor parts. Some players appear in disguise, while others are on stage for such a long time that the audience thinks they are part of the scenery. Some are hated villains, to be booed off the stage, like the Poll Tax. Others are everyday soap-opera taxes such as VAT. But the five star performers are taxes on **income**, **corporations**, **capital gains**, **sales** and **death**.

Income Tax

Income tax is paid mostly by individuals, and is a tax on income, rather than capital.

The classic distinction between capital and income is that capital is the 'tree' and income is the 'fruit'. But this is simplistic: everyone can tell an oak from an apple. It is more difficult to know whether a pile of money has come from capital growth or income. Mentioning this to tax specialists will earn you their grudging respect.

The main thing to remember in practice is that capital growth is easier to shelter from tax than income, and thus generally to be preferred.

Income tax is almost invariably banded. The names for each band will vary by country, as will their number, but the same basic principle appears almost everywhere. For example, in the UK people with very little income pay no tax at all because it is covered by **allowances**, such as the personal allowance. The next income group also pay no tax on this first slice, and pay **lower rate** tax on the next.

Most people fall into the third group, and are known as **basic rate** taxpayers. The top slice of their income is taxed at the basic rate. **Higher rate** taxpayers form the fourth and final group, and they pay all three rates of tax. Remember that top rate tax is only charged on the last slice.

A useful practical point is that the **self-employed** pay less tax than employees, given the same level of income. This is because employees are the only group in society against whom it is still legal to discriminate. Different governments have different methods, but they all discriminate.

It is, of course, easier to collect taxes from people with a regular salary than from the self-employed whose affairs are always more delicate. In some countries, such as Greece, almost all income tax is paid by government employees.

In the UK the discrimination is twofold: benefits and deductions.

1. **Benefits**

Employees may be given non-cash benefits such as company cars and health insurance. Although benefits used to save tax, a combination of new laws and inflation means that it is the taxman who now gets the benefit.

Company cars, in particular, have been targeted by legislation. Knowing this fact gives you a powerful weapon. In any business meeting mention that, as company cars are no longer tax-efficient, you have heard they will soon be replaced by a cash allowance. Most executives are so attached to their cars that you will thus be able to deflect any meeting from its original objective.

A mobile phone is an indispensable benefit for professional bluffers. (How else do you dissemble your location, or the reason you are so late home?) But rules for taxing mobile phones are so intricate and onerous that almost everyone who uses one is caught.

There are numerous other so-called benefits, all of which have to logged by employers on a Form P11D. Since the Inland Revenue gets a copy there is no point in bluffing: just check that the form is right before using it to help complete your tax return.

Should the Inland Revenue or DSS suggest you should be paying tax on some new benefit, such as:

- using the firm's photocopiers to duplicate your Christmas letters
- 'borrowing' office stationery for use at home
- calling a cousin in New York on the office phone

remind the official that there is a real world outside, and that keeping records for this type of benefit is ridiculous. The magic word here is **deregulation**. The UK government was once foolish enough to promise it would cut red tape for business. It should never be allowed to forget this.

2. **Deductions**

In Britain the self-employed can deduct expenses from their taxable income if the costs are 'wholly and exclusively' for business reasons. This means that a **dual purpose** expense cannot be claimed.

Mallalieu v Drummond is the seminal tax case here. It is one of two tax cases suitable for discussing at dinner parties. The other is *CIR v Aken (q.v)*.

Ms Mallalieu was a barrister who, like other barristers, was required to wear black in court. She always wore coloured clothes at home, so she claimed a tax deduction for her court dress. However the House of Lords decided the black clothes were not wholly and exclusively for work, but partly to 'preserve warmth and decency'. In other words, she could not go naked to court. This would have made her guilty of conduct liable to cause a breach of the peace.

Mallalieu is an extreme example. Surprisingly, the Revenue does recognise the division of some expenses. For example, if you work at home, you can claim tax relief on part of your heating bills, not to mention repairs to your waterworks.

If costs exceed income, you may have a **tax loss**, which could work in your favour if you:

a) offset it against other taxable income, such as bank interest,

b) carry it forward to reduce next year's taxable profits, or,

c) carry it back against last year's profits.

Individual tax losses are a bluffer's delight. Can you convince the Revenue that your expensive hobby is a loss-making business, and thus reduce your overall tax bill? To succeed you will need to show you tried to make profits, but if you make losses for too many years, the Inspector will call your bluff.

Some hobbies meet more resistance than others. A classic non-starter is buying and selling shares. In *Salt v Chamberlain* the taxpayer was a mathematician with computer skills, who systematically dealt on the stock exchange. However his system was unsuccessful, and he made losses. The court held he was not trading and therefore could not claim loss relief. Had he succeeded, the Revenue would have been inundated by similar sob stories.

Employees have to meet a more stringent test for expenses. Their costs must be 'wholly, exclusively and necessarily' spent in carrying out their work. Adding this one word, 'necessarily', makes the test almost impossible to meet. It means, 'necessary for everyone who does a similar job'. Thus, while you may need to buy the *Financial Times* or *Racing Post* every day to understand your clients' business, you will only get a tax deduction for the cost if it would be impossible to do your job without it. ('No F.T., no comment.')

The solution can be stage managed: get your employer to purchase what you need and give it to you. If he buys the newspaper and lets you read it, his cost is deductible because employers do not need to pass the 'necessary' test. The Revenue relies on their parsimony.

Corporate Tax

A company is a separate person in law and thus has a **legal personality**. It is therefore treated as an entity distinct from the shareholders who own it, and from the employees and directors who work for it. This separation is known as the **corporate veil**. Company law does not normally permit outsiders to lift this veil, although it can be renounced voluntarily, as in 'The Dance of the Seven...' In exchange for this privileged modesty, a company pays its own taxes.

Profits

Companies are generally taxed on their profits. The point to note is that **taxable profits** are often different from accounting profits. This is because:

a) Accounts contain round sum estimates, and these estimates are hated by tax gatherers. They like to pretend tax is an exact science, like economics.
b) Tax law requires that some amounts are calculated in a special way for tax purposes.
c) Some expenses are specifically forbidden for tax purposes. In certain countries, for example, customer entertaining is **disallowed** – a suitable excuse, if you are the host, for not buying the next round.

You therefore cannot simply take the accounting profit and multiply it by the tax rate. That would be far too straightforward.

Losses

If a company makes **taxable losses** rather than profits, **tax reliefs** provide a consolation prize for shareholders. The rules vary by country, but generally a loss can be used to reduce some or all of the following:

1. Future taxable profits of the company.

2. Past taxable profits of the company. This is better than the first option because you recover tax paid in earlier years, usually with interest.

3. Taxable profits of other companies owned by the same shareholders. For this to be possible, the tax system must treat such companies as a group for tax purposes. These are known as **group relief** provisions, and are necessary if you want to play premier league tax games.

Tax losses thus have their uses. If you are responsible for the loss in the first place, knowing this may save your bacon.

Small and Close

There are two interesting corporate tax variants: **small** companies and **close** companies. Some are small and some are close. Some very cuddly ones are both small and close.

A close company is one with relatively few shareholders. Special, complex tax rules apply to close companies, but you don't have to know them, as long as you remember that they are 'close', not 'closed'.

A small company is one which has relatively low profits and turnover. It is thus taxed at the basic rate of income tax, like an individual, rather than at the higher, corporate rate. If you are involved with a company, make sure that it is being taxed at the correct rate – you might be overpaying.

In the United States, small companies are known as S Corporations. These are See-through for tax purposes, in that the shareholders' corporate veil is transparent.

Dividends

Company profits are first taxed and then paid out to shareholders as dividends. These are then taxed in the hands of the shareholders.

This double bounce troubled the conscience of some taxmen who, in an unexpected burst of compassion, invented a complicated **imputation system** to prevent the same income being taxed twice. Examples are the *avoir fiscal* in France and, in Britain, **Advance Corporation Tax** – abbreviated as ACT, pronounced A-Sea-Tea, and not 'act' as in 'double-act'. However the benefits of this relief have been reduced by recent UK Governments in order to alleviate their compassion fatigue.

Capital Gains Tax

In the beginning there was income tax, but it was too easy to avoid. For example, companies pay their profits to shareholders as dividends, which are taxed as income. If no dividend is paid, profits accumulate within the company. The shares will reflect this accumulated value, which could be realised on a sale. Income could thus be converted into a tax-free capital gain. A open goal of this sort could not be allowed. The Revenue's counter-offensive was **capital gains tax (CGT)**.

Gains can be either **realised** or **unrealised**. If you sell an asset at a profit, this is a realised gain. If the asset has gone up in value, but has not been sold, you have an unrealised gain. Such an asset can be described as 'pregnant with gains'. It means that gains exist but have not yet been delivered.

In general, capital gains taxes only bite when there is a realised gain. This is for the good practical reason that otherwise you may have no cash to pay the tax.

Exemptions

Never make the mistake of thinking that all assets are subject to CGT. Some are too trivial to bother with, such as low value antiques. Others, such as cars, are almost invariably sold at a loss, and the Revenue wants to prevent people accumulating tax losses. Decorations for gallantry are excluded because taxing them would be bad form.

Small gains, up to an annual tax-free amount, are often excluded from tax. This is because the tax is so horribly complicated, even the Revenue do not want to work out the sums.

So find out the annual exemption, and keep your gains below it. This way you never pay.

Avoiding Taxable Gains

If your gains are going to be above the limit, consider:

1. **Realising losses**. If you own other assets which are now worth less than when you bought them (i.e. have **unrealised losses**), contemplate selling them and realising the losses. This allows you to offset the losses against your gains, reducing your total taxable amount.

2. **Spouse exemption**. Your spouse has a tax-free amount too, and gifts of assets to one another are not taxed. If you give some of the assets to your spouse and he/she sells them, this will use up his/her tax-free allowance, not yours.

   There are a number of points to watch here:

   - You can only transfer assets, not gains. So if you have already sold the assets, it's too late.
   - Your spouse has to sell the assets freely and must be able to keep the money. If you require him/her to sell, or the money goes into your bank account, the Revenue may challenge the transfer as a fake.
   - If your marriage is under strain, transfers are dicey. A gift of several thousand pounds may improve the relationship, but equally it may fund your spouse's clandestine assignations.

3. **Bed and breakfast**. In tax terms this means selling shares at the end of one day and buying them back first thing the next.

   If you have unrealised losses, but want to go on owning the shares, bed and breakfasting allows you to realise the loss, but hang on to the asset.

   One question to ask before checking into a B&B

is, "What are the transaction costs?" In other words, how much will you have to pay the stockbroker for selling your shares at dusk one day and buying them back at first light the next? The question alone may help to keep the charges down.

Bed and breakfasting can only be done easily with shares or similar assets. Don't try it with your holiday home. It is quicker and more tax-efficient to turn this into a real B&B.

Calculating Gains

If you are finding your CGT position difficult, be grateful. You are rich beyond most people's wildest dreams. Employ a professional, and keep him on his toes by asking if he has considered:

- **Losses**. These can be set against gains, effectively increasing the total tax-free amount.

- **Transaction costs**. Most costs of buying and selling the asset are allowable for tax.

- **Enhancement costs**. If you have been duped into installing double glazing or attaching a conservatory to your holiday home, console yourself by claiming tax relief on their cost.

- **Inflation**. In many countries the original cost of the asset can be increased by an inflation factor. For example, if inflation has been 5% over the period of ownership, the cost is increased by 5%. This means that the taxable gain is less. The word to use here is **indexation**. The theory is that you should not be taxed on a **paper gain**, i.e. an increase in value which is solely due to inflation. The Revenue do try to be fair sometimes.

Inflation is calculated according to a government Retail Price Index (**RPI**). This is based on what a two-adult, two-child family would spend on normal daily living. The family is a romantic fiction, but so is comparing the price of a basket of household foods with stock market movements or house prices. In short, the inflation calculation is a bit of a joke, but generally one which is on your side.

Value Added and Sales Tax

VAT is a chain letter. This is how it works:

1. A forester cuts down a tree, sells the wood to a carpenter, and adds VAT to the sale price.

2. The carpenter makes a bookcase, adding VAT to his sale price. The key point to remember is that he doesn't pay all this VAT to the government. He first deducts the tax he paid the woodcutter when he bought the wood. Hence the tax he pays is only on the value he has added to the wood. (Note that this applies even if no value has been added, such as repairing an antique).

3. The chain continues, from carpenter to distributor, from distributor to shopkeeper. Each pays some VAT.

4. But all chain letters have a victim, usually the unsuspecting man in the street. VAT is no different. The one who buys the bookcase and takes it home pays tax on the full cost, and can deduct nothing.

Sales taxes in many countries operate in exactly the same way. In some the system is less sophisticated, with tax only charged at the final stage, the sale to the consumer. But even then their similarities to VAT are greater than their differences. In particular:

- Both are **regressive**: the less you earn, the bigger the share of your income it takes. This is the opposite of income taxes, which are **progressive**.

- Both are **indirect taxes**, making leakage from wallets less obvious. This is why they are favoured by governments which have an impossible programme of tax cuts: they reduce the **headline rate** of direct tax, while indirect taxes are surreptitiously notched up.

- Both are collected by business people who are press-ganged into being unpaid VAT collectors. Don't ever underestimate the amount of time the paperwork takes. It is the sting in the tail of self-employment.

One of the problems with VAT is that it does not apply to everything. Each country has at least two rates, and deciding which rate applies keeps Eurocrats' minds fully exercised. In the UK, although food has a zero rate of VAT, some particularly delicious edibles are not classified as food, but as luxuries. So biscuits are food, but chocolate isn't. Thus assorted biscuits count as food provided they have less than 15% chocolate content – which is why there are never enough chocolate biscuits in the tin.

There are also some goods and services, such as banking and insurance, which are exempt from VAT. It is very easy to go wrong at this point, by assuming that exemption is a good thing. Normally it is. If you are exempt from corporation tax or CGT, you don't pay it. But VAT is different: if you are exempt from VAT you cannot charge VAT to your customers. But you still have to pay VAT to your suppliers, and will not be allowed to recover it.

Care is also needed to distinguish exemption from zero-rating. If you manufacture plain biscuits, they are zero rated, and you do not have to charge VAT when you sell them. However you can also reclaim all the VAT that was included in your purchases. Thus, instead of paying VAT, Customs will send you a tax refund. This is the ideal position, and the complete opposite of being exempt.

Small businesses with a low turnover do not need to charge VAT at all. This is a good thing, but an audacious bluffer may do even better. If you are selling zero-rated goods, **voluntary registration** allows you to reclaim the VAT suffered on your purchases. Freely agreeing to come within a tax sounds risky, but it is no more dangerous than the eyes on a butterfly's wing. You recover money from Customs, and administration is your only cost.

Death Duties

Death duties, like death itself, have many euphemisms – Inheritance Tax (**IHT**), Estate Duty, Probate Duty and Capital Transfer Tax. But they all mean the same. It is the Revenue's revenge for reducing the taxpaying population.

Dead people can't complain or vote and so are easy to tax. The Roman Emperor Augustus was the first to realise this. He sent tax collectors to the homes of the newly deceased to pick over their possessions. The collectors stamped *'Requiescat in pace'* or R.I.P., on anything they did not fancy, and beneficiaries had to settle for the left-overs.

In most tax systems part of the deceased's possessions can still be passed on without tax. For example, in many countries bequests to spouses are partly or wholly tax free. Small estates also escape, for a very practical reason: the tax costs too much to collect.

The combination of death and taxes worries people. Don't be thrown by it. Inheritance planning is difficult; after all, only suicides know the key date, and few people are prepared to go to such lengths even to save tax. In any case, most inheritance tax schemes are invalidated by suicide, because otherwise they would be too easy to effect.

Serious inheritance tax planning involves complicated legal webs woven to trap some of the deceased's money and prevent it falling into the taxman's hands. Despite the Revenue, who instinctively distrust these trust-based schemes, they are generally successful – because most of the money ends up in the hands of the lawyers.

Such complex schemes are in any event unnecessary, unless you are very rich. Most bluffers only need to consider:

1. Being generous now. Gifts made by the living are partly or wholly tax free.

2. Buying a life insurance policy to fund death duties.

3. Leaving everything above the exempt amount to your spouse. This is tax free because it is thought that, even with a significant financial incentive, married people will not kill each other. Sometimes this optimism is misplaced.

4. Staying alive as long as possible, thus delaying collection of the tax.

MINOR CHARACTERS

National Insurance Contributions

In the UK the most interesting minor player is itself a bluffer. National Insurance Contributions (**NIC**) is an income tax disguised as an entitlement to state benefits.

Under NIC you pay 'contributions', and receive in turn various allowances, payable when times are hard – if you lose your job, fall ill, or become pregnant. In reality the link is very slight. The word 'contribution' is particularly misleading, implying as it does that the tax is voluntary.

There are several types of NIC, some paid by employers, and others by employees. The self-employed have two specific classes, while company cars have a sub-class all to themselves.

NICs are ignored by many tax specialists as beneath their dignity, and you can follow their example. However, they can come in useful at difficult meetings about salary and benefit changes. The simple question, 'How will this change affect the NIC position?' trips up most personnel managers and allows employees time to regroup.

Property Taxes

These are also known as taxes on **real property**. It would be reasonable to think this name reflects the fact that houses are tangible measures of wealth. In fact real means 'fixed', as distinct from property which can be carried around in a briefcase.

An Englishman's home may be his castle, but he still has to pay council tax on it – and possibly business rates as well. Local property taxes tend to be crude, and have always been based on rough estimations of value. In an earlier century property values were estimated by counting the windows. Bricking them up was commonplace, condemning residents to the gloom of a shady tax avoidance scheme.

Stamp Duty

Stamp duty is a tax on documents, not on philately. It is a widespread and ancient tax, little changed from the 19th century. You pay your tax and your document is stamped by the Controller of Stamps.

If a transaction involves no documents, there is no tax. This suggests that stamp duty is optional, because it can be avoided by simply doing without the document. However the sanction lies elsewhere: only stamped documents can be produced as evidence of ownership in a court of law. So if you ever need to take tenants to court for non-payment of rent, or prove title to your house, stamping the document stops the other side calling your bluff.

Stamp duty sticks to shares, trusts and property. When involved in a transaction concerning any of these, there are a few pertinent questions to ask your solicitor or accountant. You don't need to know the answers, that's their job.

- Is there any stamp duty? Forgetting it can be costly.

- What is the rate of duty? Good words to remember here are *ad valorem* (a percentage of the asset's market value), and fixed. Fixed duty is generally low and therefore preferable.

- Is there a way round it? Because it is a tax on documents, there may be a method of carrying out the deal without paying duty at all, by moving from *ad valorem* to fixed. However anti-avoidance rules apply to some stamp duty schemes, so be careful.

– What is the interaction with VAT?

– What about **Stamp Duty Reserve Tax**? This obscure tax replaces stamp duty on some transactions, and is a good follow-up question if the solicitor has finessed or bluffed the previous one.

Other Taxes

Airport taxes are widespread. Like most indirect taxes, they slip insidiously into the cost, and only the most alert travellers notice their increased ticket price.

Cars are heavily taxed almost everywhere, as is **fuel**. As so many goods need to travel by road, these taxes feed through into the price of goods. So a bicycle is only partly effective as a tax-avoidance device.

To encourage recycling, **landfill taxes** are levied on those who dump rubbish, such as chemical companies, rubble removers and tree surgeons. Garbage is classified and then taxed by weight (though there is a special exemption for burying pets). Evading this tax is expensive as there is no upper limit on the penalty. Customs believe that where there's muck there's money.

Some countries have **net worth taxes**. In France the super-rich have to pay tax based on a percentage of their total wealth. This is a small cost compared to the other taxes they are doubtless avoiding: how else do they remain so rich?

TAX RELIEFS

Like the original 'good news, bad news' joke, governments commonly impose tax with one hand and take it away with the other.

If you ever undress a tax adviser, you will find tax reliefs up his sleeve. These are produced like a dramatic conjuring trick, usually shortly after he tells you his chargeable hourly rate.

You may be unusually lucky and qualify for **quick succession relief**, a reduction in the inheritance tax payable if a person's death is quickly followed by that of a beneficiary. But this is relatively uncommon: few people die from a surfeit of pleasure. **Rollover relief** is more likely. This allows you to roll the gain you have made selling one asset into another. The secret of success is never to let the gap between one disposal and the next acquisition be too long – a simple feat for anyone practised in the art of serial relationships.

Holdover relief is more temporary than rollover relief. After a certain period it wears off. This is especially true if a **wasting asset** is involved, which, regrettably, it all too often is. In tax terms a wasting asset is one which diminishes naturally, such as a lease.

If it all becomes too exhausting, you may be entitled to **retirement relief**. This allows you to dispose of the whole business, while paying little or no tax. To qualify, you must be over 50. It is important to note that the name itself is a bluff – you don't actually have to retire but can still go on working, as long as you sell your original business.

Each country has its own system of tax reliefs. It is possible to do a round-the-world tax-relief tour, but before you set out check the latest tax agents' updates. Recommendations include:

- Holidaying in Hong Kong, where the costs are tax-deductible.
- Procreating in France, with its 'nursery to university' child-related reliefs.
- Being idle in Spain, so avoiding the Activity Tax.
- Being mean in the US, which taxes many gifts.
- Buying a tax-deductible wardrobe in Japan, after an earthquake has swallowed the first.
- Falling ill in Germany, where the costs are allowable.
- Dying in Italy, where tax relief can be claimed on your funeral.

In reality some reliefs are so small as to be an embarrassment. The UK gives a tiny tax allowance to the blind and an even smaller one to widows. New Zealand has a housekeeper allowance which will just about cover the cost of a week's tea and biscuits. Germany allows a scarcely visible deduction for church taxes and charitable donations.

At the other end of the scale, **capital allowances** are an important tax relief. Most tax systems have capital allowances, a.k.a. '**tax depreciation**'. Key facts are:

- They are available on **capital assets**, broadly those with an expected life of at least two years.

- A percentage of the purchase cost can be deducted from taxable income for each year you use the asset in your business. The percentage is almost invariably set by the government, though ships have '**free depreciation**', so their owners can choose how much to deduct each year. This generosity stops them sailing away to a better tax regime.

- They are available to those who use an asset for their work.

- Allowances can be claimed on industrial buildings (IBAs) or plant and machinery.

IBAs only apply to buildings which could have existed at the time of Queen Victoria, such as mills, factories, canals, tunnels, bridges and tea plantations, plus shelters for cereal-threshers and ploughmen.

All attempts to bring these tax reliefs out of the 19th century to cover offices, banks, or retail shops have been rejected. It would make them both too expensive and too useful.

Plant and machinery allowances are more widely available than IBAs and also more generous. The Revenue thus has an even greater incentive to reduce claims, but has to rely on its own initiative rather than the legislation. Its chief weapon is 'continuous assessment', an examination method where the league tables change each year, which makes it more and more difficult to qualify.

Hundreds of cases on capital allowances have come to court. Many tell you little about tax but a lot about taxpayers' persistence and ingenuity. For example, the Revenue have succeeded in proving that stallions, wallpaper pattern books, floating restaurants, quarantine kennels, and inflatable tennis court covers are *not* plant and machinery.

On the other hand, detailed analysis of almost any building will produce a list of hidden assets which are allowable. Hot water pipes, lavatories, basins, lifts and moveable partitions are all eligible. If you want to unsettle a property manager or tax accountant, ask if he's comfortable that all available capital allowances have been claimed. Then sit back and watch him squirm.

Playing House

Because there is no place like home, it has special tax treatment.

- If you borrow money to buy a house, some of the interest may be tax deductible.

- Any capital gain made when you sell your home is generally not taxed. If you have two houses in the UK, you can choose which of them is your main home for CGT. This doesn't have to be the same property as the one for which you are claiming interest relief. By swapping backwards and forwards, combined with careful use of exemptions, a person with two houses may avoid CGT altogether. This compensates for double gardening and housework.

- In the UK, letting rooms in your house can be tax free if the rent is less than a given limit. This is called **rent-a-room** relief, but requires a legitimate tenant. Use by the hour might constitute a brothel. Despite being illegal, this is fully taxable.

- Going away and letting your whole house can be very tax efficient. In the UK, all your mortgage interest plus a range of expenses are deductible from rental income. Again, with the right timing, it is possible to avoid any CGT when you sell the house, even if you have hardly lived in it yourself.

- Letting out one house while living in another is another good ruse, especially if the let property is a **holiday home**, to which especially generous tax reliefs apply. This ensures plenty of weekend holiday cottages for flexi-time Inspectors who can leave work before the rush hour.

TAX PLANNING

People feel about tax the way they feel about sex. They are afraid they are missing out and that if they knew the right secrets they could do better: they could protect their money from the taxmen.

Like all myths, it is partly true.

Minimising tax is 1% destiny and 99% design. It is destiny to be born in the Cayman Isles, with no income tax, corporation tax, or inheritance tax. All the rest is planning: either off-the-shelf planning, culled from articles in Sunday newspapers, or expensive, bespoke, designer planning. But both are hopeless without one thing: money. Tax planning is not alchemy. If you have no money to start with you only have two choices:

1. Play with the benefits system instead.

2. Become a tax adviser and sell ideas to other people. Later on, when you have practised with their money, you can play the game with your own.

All tax planning should carry the warning: 'Don't let the tax tail wag the dog.' In other words, do not do something only for tax reasons. If you do, you may make the wrong decisions and lose more than you save in tax.

When playing at this level of the tax game, there are bonus points for:

- **Black holes**: areas of the board where you can place money but no-one can tax it. Profits which two countries both incorrectly believe has been taxed by the other have slipped down a black hole.

- **Loopholes**: faulty links in tax legislation which allow you legally to avoid tax.

To win at this game, you need **tax reclaims** and **tax shelters**; to win significantly, try **tax exile**; to hit the jackpot, use **international tax structures**.

Tax Reclaims

All governments are holding billions of pounds in over-collected tax. Although some periodically attempt to tell taxpayers this, we suspect them of bluffing, as the excess comes in useful when balancing the books.

The first step in tax planning is thus simple: check whether the government has any of your money. Then demand its immediate release, with tax-free interest as compensation for its wrongful imprisonment.

The source of these overpayments will vary by time and country. But it is worth reviewing the following:

- **Bank and building society interest**. Tax is commonly deducted from interest before you receive it, although non-taxpayers can ask for interest to be paid gross. In many cases people never get round to filling in the relevant form, so tax continues to be deducted from the interest before payment. This can be reclaimed.

- **The PAYE system**. This spreads tax allowances, such as the personal allowance, evenly through the year. Any break in employment may mean too much tax has been deducted during the tax year. Moving countries part-way through a tax year can have the same effect. A reclaim may help fund your round-the-world trip.

- **Income from overseas**. If this has suffered foreign tax and also been taxed in your home country, you may be entitled to recover the second tax paid.

You may also be entitled to tax reliefs and allowances in the overseas country. For example, a Frenchman with a UK rental property is eligible for a UK personal allowance, which may allow him to recover tax deducted from the rental income. This shows real savoir faire.

Tax Shelters

Tax shelters are like buses. They come past occasionally, sometimes in groups. Their timetable depends on the generosity (or the lethargy) of the government. If you don't jump on when one comes by, you may have missed the last bus and have to pay tax.

Eventually you have to get off, and your money may then become taxable. Clever planners hop on another bus as it rounds the corner, and thus delay paying tax for the duration of the next ride. Keep changing buses like this, and you might die in the passenger seat and avoid tax altogether.

Before hailing a passing tax shelter, check the fare. Charges levied by the shelter's managers may mean it is only good value if you are a higher rate taxpayer. Ask yourself: 'Can I afford to travel first-class?'

Each country has its own tax shelters. In the UK they include:

TESSAs (Tax Exempt Special Savings Accounts). This is an adults-only investment, restricted to one per person.

National Savings Certificates. Government savings products which pay tax-free interest in exchange for you trusting politicians with your money. But remember to withdraw it if war is announced.

PEPs (Personal Equity Plans). Any gains or dividends are tax free. But remember that if the PEP falls in value, there is no tax relief.

ISAs (Individual Savings Accounts) are the offspring of PEP and TESSA. Due in 1999, these will be tax-free and will hold a wide mix of assets – **isa** bit of this and **isa** bit of that. Like the fearsome children of mythology, ISAs may devour their parents.

Pension Funds. Here, money is paid into a pension fund gross, i.e. before being taxed, and once in the fund it also grows tax free. This makes it a tax shelter. Salesmen, who are trained to bluff, will say this often and very plausibly. But remember that you will pay tax on it when you retire, and that dividends (which are a major part of the income of a pension fund) are taxed before receipt. So it's more of a lean-to than a shelter.

Tax Exile

Tax has traditionally been territorial, because it is easier to collect money from people who live locally. Tax also overrides ethnic origins: a German who moves to France is caught by the French tax system.

The few exceptions to this apply whenever a government thinks it can get away with it. The US Internal Revenue Service, for example, taxes all citizens wherever they live, using its diabolic computer system, and withdraws citizenship if they don't submit. Other nations tax any assets left behind when you go abroad. But in general this principle of territoriality means that going abroad can reduce your tax bill, or even eliminate it altogether. Before you cross the border consider:

Dates. Exactly when you go abroad can make an enormous difference. Each country has different rules. You can live in Japan for up to 366 days without paying tax – as long as 183 of them are in one calendar year and 183 in the next. The UK has complex provisions to trap you if you return too often.

Definitions. The precise definition of 'resident' varies by country, and some have different definitions depending on the tax you are considering. In the UK you may be non-resident for income tax but resident for capital gains. In Austria, having a ski apartment may make you tax resident. Discovering this too late may cause a crevasse in your financial arrangements.

Destination. Don't jump out of the chip pan into the French frier. Check the tax regime in the new country before you land. Simple steps, like closing bank accounts, may make a big difference to your tax bill.

Death. The tax you pay on death may depend on domicile rather than residence. Your domicile is your original home, and it can only be changed with difficulty. Thus a Kiwi backpacker remains domiciled in the Antipodes even if he spent the last two years studying reincarnation in Tibet.

Your country of domicile may also tax your world-wide assets when you die, even though you went abroad decades before. Countries which operate a domicile system are extremely reluctant to believe anyone might choose to live anywhere else. Buying a cemetery plot overseas is, however, accepted as reasonable evidence that you don't intend to come back – at least not this lifetime.

Artificial Tax Planning Schemes

Traditional tax specialists advise clients on efficient tax planning. Others, usually merchant banks, sell artificial schemes. These are more risky, much better rewarded, and provoke the taxmen.

It is, in practice, easy to spot an artificial scheme:

- It comes with lots of jargon, mathematical diagrams and at least two legal opinions.
- The only really clear part of the documentation is the amount of money which the scheme will save, and the bank's share of this.
- It will be proprietary. This means that you won't be told anything about it until you've signed a confidentiality agreement, promising not to discuss it with anyone who might help you understand.

It is vital to realise that the team from the bank are all salesmen. The originator has been left behind in the bank's back office, where he can put his talents to better use dreaming up the next scheme.

You will keep control of the situation if you ask:

- Has the scheme been sold to anyone else? You need to know what your competitors are doing.
- Does it rely on invisibility for its success? It won't be secret for long if they have already discussed it with eighteen companies.
- What are the indirect tax implications? Merchant banks often overlook transaction taxes as they are seen as less sexy than direct taxes.
- What is the downside risk? This will make them anxious in case you understand the scheme. You need to know the risk because if it goes wrong someone's going to get the blame. Don't let it be you.
- What sort of guarantees can you give me that this will work?

INTERNATIONAL TAX

All tax is a game, but international tax is a top-level, multi-dimensional game, played for high stakes: you can win or lose millions. Its aim is to move money round the world so most of it ends up in the hands of its owners, and as little as possible leaks out on the way.

The game is played with five variables: **Vehicles**, **Passengers**, **Havens**, **Networks** and **Residences**. Because of the number of options, a tax planning structure is like a kaleidoscope. You must keep your eye on the moving patterns. For example:

- The profitability of an enterprise may not turn out as expected.
- Corporate objectives may alter.
- The law in one of the countries may change.

This need for constant review provides international tax experts with a regular income. They also have to make regular trips abroad, especially to sunny tax havens.

1. Vehicles

To move money around you need get-away vehicles. Rollers or rollerblades, boats or balloons: the choice is yours. The skill lies in picking the one best suited to your purpose: don't buy a mountain bike if you need a four-wheel drive. Forms of transport include:

Companies

These are the Ford Fiestas of international planning: universally popular, simple to operate and relatively cheap. They are therefore unlikely to attract much attention; the authorities do not pull them over unless they really misbehave.

Unlike cars, companies reproduce. Parent companies produce children, or **subsidiaries**. Each subsidiary is a separate person, but linked by share ownership to its parent.

Companies are nearly always taxed on their profits by the country in which they are resident. Residence is a separate variable in its own right.

Branches

Branches are not separate legal entities, but remain attached to the parent tree. In international tax terms this means that a branch belongs both where it is situated and where its parent is resident. For example, a French branch of an Australian company is part of the Australian company, so its profits will be taxed in Australia. But the French will also regard it as taxable in France.

This is unhelpful if the branch is profitable, but can be useful if it makes losses. If your company is setting up overseas for the first time, suggest that it begins as a branch, so start-up losses can be used by the main company. It can then convert to a subsidiary once it begins to make profits. With any luck, an idea like this will at least get you a couple of free trips abroad, allegedly to check that the proposal works in practice.

Rep(resentative) offices

Like many other reps, these are capable only of superficial relationships. If they show any sort of commitment, they immediately have to resign and become something more respectable, like a branch.

Lots of companies use reps in places with difficult or expensive tax regimes, like China. The advantage of reps is that they do not pay tax, because they are not supposed to be doing any real work.

Partnerships

If companies are parents, and reps are casual seducers, partnerships fall somewhere between the two. Partners generally define what they expect of one another rather than this being laid down by law. One of the partners can be a **sleeping partner**. This means the only business involvement is providing cash – e.g. paying the hotel bills. **Silent partners** are sleeping partners whose identity cannot be disclosed. They are thus ideal for secret affairs.

Partnerships often have no separate status in law: any tax falls on the partners as individuals. However some more enlightened countries, such as Holland, have formalised the arrangements and recognise partnerships as separate legal entities.

The fact that partnerships are seen as groups of individuals by some countries and as separate legal entities by others can be very useful. It is like a two-way mirror: the tax authorities abroad may see a German limited partnership as a group of individuals, and tax them accordingly; the German government taxes the same people as a single legal entity. The word for this sort of structure is **hybrid**. As with gardening, judicious use of hybrids is more fruitful than using only simple corporate offshoots.

2. Passengers

Some passengers are always stopped at the border. Others slip out unnoticed, hidden discreetly under the back seat or disguised as legitimate cargo.

Money is your passenger, but it travels in many guises. Its costume determines how much can be moved, and how easily. Knowledge of its 'wrappers' is useful, if only to show that you are really familiar with money in all its forms, and can be trusted to handle a lot more of it. They include:

- **Dividends**. This is the most up-front way of taking money out of a company. Tax authorities are familiar with dividends and will tax them. Sometimes this tax will fall on the shareholder, sometimes on the company, and in the worst cases, on both.

- **Interest**. If a business borrows money from abroad, it usually pays interest to the overseas lender. Note that this interest is deducted from profits before tax. Thus, if the lender is another entity within the same group, paying interest may be a way of getting money out without paying foreign tax on it.

  Taxmen tore their hair out over this for a while, and finally introduced **thin cap** rules, to stop them being follicley challenged. These restrict the amount of inter-company interest which can be deducted from profits for tax purposes.

  Taxmen may also take **withholding tax** from the interest. This means they keep back, or withhold, a slice of the interest as it slips over the border.

  Interest nevertheless remains a useful tax-planning tool. Asking, "How much debt can we get away with?" will show that you understand this, while recognising the limitations.

- **Royalties, copyrights and know-how**. If an overseas entity uses your software, publishes your book or develops your ideas, you can charge for it.

This payment is deductible before tax, and provides another way of moving pre-tax profits abroad.

But a sharp tax inspector can spot a royalty at twenty miles. He will probably impose a withholding tax, and may also ask whether it is reasonable to make the payment at all.

There is a knack to using royalties, copyrights and know-how, and it is this: never be greedy. Sliced thinly and layered over interest and dividends they make tasty morsels for international corporate treasuries.

- **Management charges**. The costs of running your complex group, with its companies, branches, partnerships and rep offices has to be paid for. Apart from anything else, your salary will be too much for any one entity to bear on its own. It will also be easier to camouflage if spread around.

  Most tax authorities accept that head-office or management charges can legitimately be shared out among the group. Your aim is to put most of the charges in the country with the highest tax rate, where they will reduce the taxable profits; the taxmen will want the opposite. Good luck.

- **Transfer pricing**. This is the hardest area for taxmen to pin down, and the most sophisticated way of stripping profits out of a country. If you sell goods or services to a sister company overseas, at what price do you sell them? Since 'profit' is sale price less cost, cost can determine profit. If you send the goods to India (a high tax country), via Bermuda (a low tax country), the goods may be sold to Bermuda cheaply, and then on-sold to India at a high price. This traps much of the profit in Bermuda en route.

Transfer pricing is the modern battleground, the tax Armageddon. No more duelling at dawn with gentlemanly Inspectors. Moving millions, even billions, of profit across borders requires a sophisticated Revenue defence system, like cruise missiles.

Like most cruises, a transfer pricing investigation is both unhurried and expensive. Its cost, in professional fees alone, can blow a huge hole in a well-planned budget.

If you work for a large multinational, you will one day have a transfer pricing investigation. Here are a few survival tips:

a) Prepare your defences. If you work in sales or finance, make sure that either you were not responsible for setting the prices, or that you can defend them.

b) Know your enemy. For example, do not mess with the IRS. The US Internal Revenue Service does not take prisoners. On the other hand, some countries' transfer pricing teams make Inspector Clouseau look professional.

c) Recruit more troops. This always helps, especially when you want to go home early or have a day off. Recruiting is much cheaper than paying outside advisers, and thus easily justified.

Do not let the hit-squads deter you completely. Done well, transfer pricing can still be an effective way of managing international tax.

- **Withdrawal**. As always, this is a method of last resort, and tends to be messy. Companies can be liquidated, branches closed down and partnerships dissolved. But withdrawal will be expensive in real terms, such as property and legal costs. And the foreign government will make one last heroic effort to tax you before departure.

The golden rule is: look before you leap. Spend a little money on market research before you invest in a country, rather than a fortune in legal fees and tax costs when you leave.

3. Tax Havens

Tax havens are mostly sunny islands like Barbados. They keep your money safe for ever – or at least until the revolution. The locals, who earn peanuts nailing shelf company nameplates to solicitors' doorways, will one day want their share of the wealth.

Tax havens can be cumbersome. Sark, for example, is known in the trade as 'the Sark Lark'. It can only be reached by boat and is frequently cut off by storms.

If Barbados is out of your price range, a good tax guide will list unexpected alternatives. Dunkirk, for instance, gives investors a tax holiday for ten years. If you do not speak French, there is always Dublin, which has a minimal 10% tax rate – and better beer.

For somewhere off the beaten track, try the Mezzogiorno, a region of southern Italy to which Rome has granted substantial tax incentives in an effort to attract family businesses other than the Mafia.

Tax authorities in developed countries dislike havens, and have tried to limit their use. Most have introduced **anti-avoidance** legislation aimed at companies who set up tax haven subsidiaries. The UK Revenue call such subsidiaries Controlled Foreign Companies or **CFCs**, and believe they are more environmentally damaging than spray cans.

4. Networks

A world wide web predates the Internet. Money and wealth are transferred around the globe via an invisible network of international tax treaties. The number of treaties possessed by each country varies: some countries are treaty-rich and some treaty-poor. Outlaw countries have no treaties at all.

Tax treaties include clauses on some or all of the following:

- Agreement on how key concepts, such as residence, are defined.
- **Double tax relief (DTR)**. Sadly, not double relief from tax. DTR prevents you being taxed in both countries on the same money.
- Reduced withholding tax on interest, dividends, royalties, and similar.
- Exchange of information. The taxmen on both sides will co-operate to catch you.

Tax havens are outlawed from this treaty system. There are no tax treaties with the Cayman Islands or Panama. This is because treaty countries do not want to make it even easier for their citizens to do business in such low tax areas.

There are however a few invaluable tax haven countries which link into the network via one or two treaties. Good tax planing uses these connections to move money to a tax haven. Finding the best sequence of treaties to effect this transfer is called **treaty-shopping**.

On your next visit to Amsterdam, discard your inhibitions and order a **Dutch sandwich**: not three in a bed, but classic treaty-shopping. The Netherlands has a large network of tax treaties. It is relatively easy to get your money to Holland, using one of the many available treaties. The country also has a treaty with its colonial offspring, the Netherlands Antilles, which is a tax haven. Once you have moved your money to Holland, you can use the Netherlands Antilles treaty to take it out again, virtually tax free.

5. Residence

If you play games with residence, remember that countries define it in different ways. The two main ones are:

1. A company is resident where it is incorporated. For example, a company set up under Mexican law is resident in Mexico.

2. A company is resident where it is managed and controlled, i.e. where the company's key decisions are made. Unlike incorporation, 'management and control' is not a black and white issue. Never forget that tax planners' favourite colour is grey.

By passing both tests, i.e. being incorporated in one and managed and controlled in another, a company can be **dual resident**, which means it is regarded as tax resident in both countries. This can have advantages: for example there may be a double deduction for expenses or interest paid, called **double-dipping**. It is more difficult (but not impossible) to fail both tests, so that the company is not resident anywhere.

But if your aim is to be offshore, it is no good spending a fortune setting up a Bermudan resident company when the directors have board meetings in a hotel at Heathrow. If they do, the company will be deemed to be managed and controlled in Britain. The directors will just have to be self-sacrificing, put the company first, and travel to Bermuda on a regular basis.

TAX PROFESSIONALS

Personalities

Tax experts belong to one of three personality types:

- **Zealots** who believe all the rules. In the Middle Ages they would have been theologians. Today most join the Inland Revenue or Customs & Excise.

- **Machiavellians** who plan complicated ways around the rules and are regarded as heretics by zealots. In an earlier century they would have been burnt at the stake.

- **Pragmatists** who negotiate practical solutions to tax problems. This is much the smallest group and should be cherished, if you are ever fortunate enough to meet one.

New recruits to the tax trade must get used to admitting in public what they do for a living. The simple statement, "I'm a tax specialist," can put an end to the liveliest conversations and produce silences in pubs. This is because the public never expects to meet certain kinds of people, such as nuns or tax specialists, in a normal social environment. They will be particularly worried if you work for the Revenue or Customs.

Although it is possible to dissemble and invent a fictitious profession, perpetrators are quickly discovered. Fake airline pilots are unmasked as soon as they meet another pilot, who usually turns out to be the local District Inspector.

Tax people are generally perceived as divided by a barbed wire fence. On one side is the **Revenue**, **Customs** and the **DSS**. On the other are **Tax Advisers** working for accountancy and legal firms or large companies. In reality people cross the fence surprisingly often, usually leaving the Revenue to join better-paid private-sector poachers.

Remember this fence-crossing before you insult the Revenue in front of your tax adviser – last week he may have worked for them. Some of his best friends will still be Tax Inspectors. Otherwise, how would he gain the inside knowledge you are paying him for?

Inland Revenue

A good Inspector and a bright professional adviser relate to each other like First World War flying aces and their opposite numbers. This is as close as most tax specialists get to being a pilot. The Inland Revenue is an enemy, but one worthy of respect.

This is partly because of their rigorous Civil Service training. It would be unkind to say that Inspectors are those who are left behind when MI5 have picked out the best and brightest. But many are secret agents manqué, loving the thrill of undercover investigation – even if it is only fraud and false accounting in a Chinese takeaway.

Tax cases are a key part of an Inspector's training. Inspectors know hundreds, even thousands, of cases. One of the highest accolades in the Revenue is to get your name on a major case so the next generation have to learn it. Rarer still is the Revenue equivalent of the Cheltenham double, seen in *Stokes v Costain* and *Ensign Tankers [Leasing] Ltd v Stokes*. Less successful Inspectors buy personalised number plates.

There are many advantages to employing an ex-Inspector. He will have lots of practical experience, and great contacts. But he may want to go home at five, and at noon on Fridays.

Customs & Excise and the DSS

Both Customs and the DSS are part-timers. Customs' first responsibility is to catch smugglers. They may need a reminder that legitimate VAT planning arrangements are not in the same league.

Customs are less intellectual than the Revenue, and survive on a diet of internal leaflets. In some cases their knowledge is thin to the point of anorexia. If you read the legislation, you may surprise them.

The DSS's day job is giving out benefits. Collecting National Insurance Contributions is a hobby, looked after by a branch called the Contributions Agency.

This amateurism has both advantages and disadvantages. The Agency can be infuriatingly slow when it comes to making decisions, and they have an appeals system that makes China look democratic. On the other hand they can be charmingly helpful on audit visits, overlooking mistakes and misclassifications in a way that would shock an Inspector of Taxes.

(A word of caution here: the Agency are fighting a rearguard action to prevent themselves being swallowed up by the Revenue. They are very sensitive to suggestions that this is inevitable. Their strongest argument for survival is that merging would be a false economy, as their redundancies would double the DSS's workload on the benefits side.)

Tax Advisers

Most firms of lawyers and accountants employ tax specialists: it is cheaper than buying the skills outside. Some advisers work on their own, as sole practitioners, or gather together in pairs or packs called partnerships.

Most professional firms are hierarchical, which means only partners get offices and the rest are open-plan. The hierarchy includes:

Tax Partner: Spends most of his time keeping clients happy rather than reading new rules, so is an inveterate bluffer.

Tax Group Manager: Draws lines for trainees to keep their toes on, takes them out for drinks and checks timesheets.

Tax Consultant: Marketeer. Sells tax ideas without bothering to tell clients what will happen when the Revenue discovers the full picture. Similar to a chef who doesn't wash up.

Tax Manager: Workhorse.

Tax Senior: Learning to be a workhorse, dreaming of being a partner.

Tax Accountants in industry are rarely recruited by the professional firms, as they would introduce fresh air and raise clouds of dust. On the other hand, tax people often travel in the opposite direction and move from the profession to companies. This is like leaving a convent: few return to the habit.

Buying Tax Advice

Although it is generally illegal to practice as a lawyer, doctor or auditor without the relevant qualifications, in many countries any bluffer can set up as a tax specialist. If you need a job, this is perfect. If you need advice, stage a beauty parade. Run your eye along the line up. Look for:

- **A slimline organisation**. Too much fat finds its way into the fees.

- **Previous experience**. Virgins have to learn on the job and this is expensive.

- **Long term potential**. The relationship has to survive as you change and grow.

- **Last minute substitutions**. The attractive charismatic partner moves on to the next client.

Another way of assessment is to compare the adviser to a geographer. The latter does not know every detail about a country, but he knows the lie of the land.

The same is true of a good tax specialist. He may not have done any inheritance tax for years, but he knows that if you leave a gift to charity in your will, some very nasty calculations follow. In other words, he has a tax atlas in his head. When you ask a question he knows the location of the answer, if not its postcode. He will also tell you if he does not know the answer. Always remember that you are the bluffer.

When aeroplanes crash, rescuers look for the black box. Company directors treat tax in the same way, and wait till something goes wrong before getting involved. Be different. Try asking:

- For a summary of the tax consequences for all major transactions.
- What the cost will be. This will be good news for most advisers, who waste hours later on trying to extract fees. Since the cost of this time is invariably added to the next bill, agreeing an estimate up-front immediately reduces this overhead.
- Whether there is an alternative. Tax people are always saying they are creative: let them prove it.

Accounting for Tax

There is only one essential fact to remember about Tax Accounting. It is not tax. It is an estimate of the tax payable which is included in the year end accounts.

Because it's not tax, tax specialists look down on it. This includes the Revenue. Although company accounts are sent to the tax office, they are accompanied by a return or computation which calculates the tax payable on a more exact basis. Never worry too much what the tax charge is in your accounts. The Inspector will hardly ever ask you why it is twice as big as the number in your computation. This condescension is fortunate.

There are two common reasons why the numbers are so different:

1. Lots of borderline reliefs and exemptions have been deducted in your computation, but the Inspector may realise they are borderline and challenge them. Accountants, being prudent, insist on these being ignored for the accounts.

2. Some items can be deducted immediately in the accounts, but must be spread for tax purposes. This is called a **timing difference**. Accounts have to be adjusted for timing differences, and this is done by setting up artificial or **deferred** tax. Deferred tax is irreconcilably difficult. Defer to the specialists: it is their job to balance the books.

Profit before tax (**PBT**) is the accountants' revenge for being despised by tax specialists. Accountants believe tax is a fixed cost, and thus it is the profit before tax which reflects how well the organisation has performed against competitors.

Worse, they have persuaded market analysts that this is true.

This view is deeply insulting to tax specialists, whose lives are dedicated to reducing the tax charge. Calling tax a fixed cost undermines the specialists' whole raison d'être, and devalues their contribution to a company's profitability.

Concentrating on profit before tax to the exclusion of the actual tax paid can be very costly. Accountants who deal with fictitious rolling budgets and round sum estimates often forget that tax paid leaves the company's coffers for ever. It cannot be adjusted next year like an accounting entry.

Actuaries are even worse than accountants at this. They live in an arcane area called a reserve, to which access is restricted. In these enclosures they play with huge artificial numbers, completely losing touch with everyday realities, such as cash.

UNDERSTANDING TAX LAW

Most religions are split into two factions. One follows the text of the scriptures, interpreting its exact words and comparing them internally, rather like literary criticism. The other seeks to express the heart of the religious message, and sees the scriptures as helpful, but not ultimately authoritative.

Taxation is similarly divided between those who follow the words of the legislation and others who try to discover what the legislation was intended to do. We can call the first the literal school and the second the purposive school.

The UK and most of its ex-colonies follow the first approach. Europe generally takes a more purposive line. Both have advantages and disadvantages. The literal approach gives greater certainty: if the law says X then X will apply. The disadvantage is that making X apply in these circumstances may be non-sense, and clearly not what Parliament meant.

In either case, tax law can be sub-divided into rules. It is not always easy, however, to know which rules apply to you. This may be because your situation is unusual. But this is unlikely. The more probable reasons are that:

- You cannot find out what the rules are.

- You can find the rules but they are incomprehensible.

- The rules are not being followed in practice.

The core of UK law is parliamentary legislation or **statute law**. Its gaps are glossed over until someone gets into an argument with the Revenue and one or other of them takes a case to court. The decisions of the judges form **case law**.

If the Revenue loses a case, it has the power and

influence to get the statute changed. Usually this type of change is accompanied by an announcement that the change 'puts the law back where everyone thought it was'.

Mostly this behaviour is tolerated, unless the Revenue announce that the new legislation is **retrospective**. This means that they have effectively unpicked the court's decision. Retrospection is generally regarded as overstepping the mark.

Even the Revenue recognise that tax law is a foreign language, and publish their interpretations as **Statements of Practice**. To top it all, government departments also issue **regulations**.

The tax rule on a particular point may thus be an amalgam of case law, statute, regulation and interpretation. This is why tax advisers cover their letters with caveats. Don't accept them. You pay for advice, not bluff.

Accessibility

If you want to solve a tax problem, knowing where to start is not easy. Even bluffers need a few facts to hide behind. We recommend:

- **Revenue pamphlets**. These have the advantage of being free, but the disadvantage that they won't point out any weaknesses in the taxman's case.

- **Tax annuals**. These are found in public libraries, and are easier to get hold of than *The Beano*. Never, ever read last year's annual. It is dangerous and can seriously damage your wealth.

- **Free literature**. Most major accounting and law firms publish free booklets highlighting changes to tax law. Call their head office and ask for the

Publications Department. Don't worry that you're not a client or even a potential client. Ask confidently for an up-to-date list of leaflets and tick off what you want. Make sure your name goes on the mailing list; this way you keep your phone bill down.

- **Revenue manuals**. As part of a campaign for open government, these can be found at the tax office. They include summaries of the Revenue's approach to tax law and practice. But you won't find everything in the manuals: they may be open but they're not wide open.

Taxspeak

Tax legislation is written by draftsmen who never use three sentences when one will do. For example:

> *'Where the relief to which a person is entitled for any year of assessment consists in an income tax reduction calculated by reference to a specified amount, the effect of that relief shall be that the amount of that person's liability for that year to income tax on his total income shall be the amount to which he would have been liable apart from that provision less whichever is the smaller of—*
> *a) the amount equal to 20% of the specified amount;*
> *b) the amount which reduces his liability to nil.'**

If you can't understand a letter you receive, refer the Inspector to his own Complaints Manual. It's your right as a taxpayer to prefer plain vanilla English.

---

*Translation: Certain personal allowances create a 20% tax credit, but this cannot be repaid to an individual unless he has sufficient taxable income.

Forms

Tax and forms go together like eggs and spoons, stories and journalists. One is a necessary to extract the other.

There are so many tax forms that the only reasonable course of action is to ask: "Is there a separate form for that?" whenever something new comes up. The chances are there will be. By asking you will get a gold star for good behaviour on your tax file, and make penalties less likely.

People who never have to fill in a tax form are enviable creatures, like thin people who never have to diet. Membership of this charmed circle is open only to those whose income has been fully taxed before receipt, such as salary paid under PAYE, and UK bank or building society interest.

The Revenue will send you a form if they think you have more tax to pay. But they are not the know-alls they would have us believe: their standard tool-kit does not yet include a crystal ball. So if you have received income which has not been fully taxed, you are not allowed to blame the taxman for not sending you a tax form. You have to ask for it, painful though this is.

Codes

It is no accident that tax reference numbers are known as **codes**. Decipher your reference number and you can discover how much tax you will pay during the year under the PAYE system. But these codes are a bluff: they are too easy to decipher to be taken seriously. The real enigma is the legislation itself, known in the trade as 'The Code'. Break this and they will take you seriously.

Self Assessment

Everyone in Britain has now been hectored into **SA**, or Self Assessment. Like self-analysis and self-help it originated in the USA, although a similar system exists in Australia and France. SA also stands for Sex Appeal. The similarities are startling:

1. Both mark the passage from childhood to adulthood. Under SA, taxpayers take responsibility for their own returns: they can no longer blame their employer or the Revenue.

2. Despite hundreds of articles in the press, no-one really understands how either work.

3. Both carry risks and penalties, and cause unexpected misunderstandings.

4. In a thorough investigation, midnight raids occur.

However, while Sex Appeal depends on shape, Self Assessment depends on forms. These arrive in April. If you miss the 30 September cut-off date, you will have to fill in the forms and calculate the tax due. If you haven't done so, and paid the tax by the following 31 January, you will suffer interest and penalties.

The only way out is a 'reasonable excuse' such as life-threatening illness or burglars stealing your books of account. Pressure of work, ignorance, poverty or holidays abroad are no protection once you have entered the penalty zone.

But if you play their game and send the relevant information to the Revenue by 30 September, they will calculate your tax, and tell you what to pay, just as they did before. Although this Revenue calculation is also called Self-Assessment, it is not. SA is thus an enormous Revenue bluff.

AVOIDING AND EVADING

It is important to distinguish avoiding tax from its evasion. There is a marked difference.

Tax Avoidance

Tax avoidance means using the existing law to reduce your tax bill. The key principle is that no-one '*is under the smallest obligation, moral or other, so to arrange his legal relations to his business or to his property as to enable the Inland Revenue to put the largest possible shovel into his stores*'. This useful quotation comes from the case of *Ayrshire Pullman Motor Services & Ritchie v CIR*.

If you organise your affairs so the Revenue have to use the smallest possible shovel, quote the case of *Duke of Westminster v CIR*. In this the judge said that everyone '*is entitled if he can to order his affairs so that the tax attaching under the appropriate Acts is less than it otherwise would be*'.

You need to be aware, however, that this Westminster principle has its limitations, introduced because taxpayers, like teenagers, pushed the rules as far as they could. So elaborate were the avoidance schemes that the courts decided the Westminster principle would not apply if there were:

a) a pre-planned series of transactions

b) steps inserted into the transactions which had no business purpose other than tax avoidance.

When the Revenue know that you can legally avoid tax, they tend to introduce **anti-avoidance** legislation to prevent you. If something sounds too good to be true, ask: "What about anti-avoidance legislation?".

Even if you are told none exists, be warned: it can be introduced overnight. This may catch you with your fiscal trousers down.

Tax Evasion

Tax evasion means you have deliberately not paid tax. If you are found out, you will have to pay large sums of back tax, interest and penalties, and your file will be marked with a sticker saying, 'WATCH THIS ONE'. In the most serious cases, you may go to jail. This is not a bluff.

Investigation

It is very unpleasant to be investigated by the Revenue or Customs, especially if they suspect you of evasion.

If you are being investigated, your first question is always 'Why?' These are some of the answers:

- You have been moonlighting, and advertised your skills in the local paper. The Revenue read it.
- You suppressed some cash takings from your business, and as a result your profits are lower than the Revenue/Customs would expect. Both organisations have detailed studies for most types of business, showing normal profits and the key variable factors.
- Something unusual in your tax return has prompted a tax official to ask questions.
- Taxmen have posed as customers, and had dinner in your restaurant. They then checked whether their payment went into the books. The food portions you served may also have been used as a

statistical sample to see if the profit margin on the meal matches that in your accounts.
- Someone has sneaked on you.
- A bank has reported your savings interest to the Revenue. This is cross-checked to your tax return.
- Your lifestyle doesn't match your declared earnings.

As well as being investigated because of Revenue suspicions, you may also be the subject of a random audit. This means you have been selected on a statistical basis: a sort of reverse National Lottery.

The trouble is, no-one will tell you this, so you won't know whether the investigation is random or targeted. Keep records. You may need to prove where that money in your bank account came from.

At the other end of the spectrum from random audits, special investigation teams deal with the **Phoenix** and **Ghost**. This is not a real ale pub. A phoenix is a company which goes into liquidation, owing tax and VAT debts, and then starts up again under another company name. Ghosts are people who, as far as the tax office records are concerned, don't exist.

Justification

When called to see the taxman, the first reaction is to make excuses, such as:

- 'I won the money in the lottery.' This is so common that some countries have a black market in winning lottery tickets – after the winnings have been paid out to the original holder.
- 'I won it on the horses.' ("Show us your slips.")
- 'I inherited it from an elderly distant aunt who lived abroad.' ("Name her.")

- 'It's just a hobby and I don't make much.' ("How much?")

Do not try to argue that you should not be taxed because what you are doing is outside the law. In the tax case of *CIR v Aken* a prostitute argued she could not be taxed because if she was, the Crown would be living on immoral earnings. She failed, presumably because the morality of most of the Crown's income has historically always been dubious.

Complaining

The Code requires the Revenue to reimburse your costs if they have made mistakes or been late getting back to you. Note that the Revenue idea of a delay is seven months – when they are writing the letters. If you take that long to reply, expect to be raided.

Mistakes include situations where the taxman has:

- Taken a 'wholly unreasonable' view of the law.
- Continued to ask questions about 'obviously trivial matters'.
- Ignored you when you corrected a Revenue mistake.
- Made a trivial mistake which could lead to far more serious consequences.
- Cannot stop making mistakes.

If this has happened to you, send the Revenue a bill for your expenses, including any lost earnings. You can also ask for a 'consolatory payment' as compensation for your distress.

The **Taxpayers' Charter** is a good scare tactic. It strikes terror into those who have not been 'fair, helpful, efficient and accountable' and is taken very seriously by Ministers. You may also wish to consider the **Revenue Adjudicator** whose sole purpose in life is to examine complaints from taxpayers and recommend solutions. Asking for the Adjudicator's address from your local DI may help focus his mind.

Negotiation

The Revenue wants you to pay tax and you object. Try negotiation: you may end up with a lower settlement. But it will only work if the Revenue believe you have something they want – apart, of course, from lots of tax.

Your objective is to persuade the Revenue that you are holding at least one of the following cards. Play them close to your chest:

- You believe there is some technical flaw in either the evidence itself or the Revenue interpretation of the evidence. Whether there is or not doesn't matter too much. If you can give a convincing display of your doubts, you may persuade a court.

- You will fight this case to the bitter end. Penniless debtors cannot pay tax. Also the DSS will be upset at the extra costs of maintaining your family.

- You will demand compensation and costs when you win. This will worry them. Their expense claim might be rejected by the Treasury. Worse still, it might go on their P11D.

- You have some information they want, perhaps on how a tax avoidance scheme works. If you tell them, they will save investigation time and can move on to the next case.

- If you settle the tax now, they'll have it by the end of March. This is the end of the Revenue's financial year. Taxmen have performance targets too.

GLOSSARY

Assessment – What you think of the Revenue.

ATII – Abbreviation for: a) member of the Chartered Institute of Taxation; b) 'All Tax Is Impossible', 'All Tax Is Impenetrable' and 'Any Tax Is Immoral'.

Back Duty – Investigation of unpaid tax. More painful than a slipped disc.

Benefits in kind – Earnings paid in goods rather than cash. Used to be kind to the pocket, but now so only at the margin; thus 'fringe' benefits.

Bond – Written acknowledgement of a loan to a company, which can be sold on the stock market. Bonds usually have numbers for security reasons, hence 007.

Bond washing – Tax avoidance device for turning income into capital gains by selling the bond before interest is received. The interest is thus included in the gain rather than being taxed as income. Effective bond-washing allows you to clean up.

Bracket creep – Tendency to be pushed into the next tax band by inflation, rather than because of increased real income. (Sycophantic inspectors recognise this but prefer to hide it in parentheses.)

Captive – Bank or insurance subsidiary company in a tax haven. The Revenue may hold the parent hostage until some profits are released.

Charge – The sudden and rapid collection of a tax. Avoidance may be fatal, as in the Charge of the Light Brigade.

Concession – Relaxation of the law in your favour, unless you're a tax avoider. Concessions never give rights to a gold mine.

Connected persons – Most relatives of a taxpayer, plus maids, but excluding lovers and mistresses.

Customs – First cousins of the Revenue, so-called because of their strange habits.

Day – 24 hours ending at midnight. A visit to the UK beginning at 9 a.m. and ending at 5 p.m. the same day is thus deemed never to have happened.

Death – The only other great certainty, now undermined by cryogenics.

Deem – Revenue-speak for 'Let's pretend'.

DI – Inspector who runs the District and is Divinely inspired; like the Pope but with slightly more authority.

Distress – Customs seize your goods. Very upsetting.

Excise – To take out. What happens if you get on the wrong side of your VAT Inspector.

Gross – Paid before deduction of tax, or excessive tax.

Higher paid – An employee who earns more than £8,500 p.a. Indicator of Revenue salary levels.

Interest – Shown by the Revenue if you don't declare all your bank accounts.

MIRAS – Greek God who nibbles at tax reliefs until they're invisible to the naked eye.

Net – Payment after deduction of tax. Previously used for fishing smuggled goods out of ponds. Customs today prefer muckraking to moonraking.

Offshore – Any country where the tax is less than at home. Regarded as offside by the Revenue.

Paradis fiscal – French for tax haven.

PAYE – Pay All You Earn.

Ring fence – Separate and isolate for tax purposes. Similar to ring roads which separate drivers from their destination and isolate town centres.

Schedule D – Tax rules applying to the self-employed. 'D' stands for 'doubtful', 'deceptive', 'defective' and 'defraud'.

Schedule E – Tax rules applying to employees. 'E' stands for 'expensive'.

Tax holiday – Period of freedom from tax.

Tax reliefs – What some people collect in the belief that they will ensure eternal life for their wealth, like medieval indulgences.

Tax Year – One which begins in the UK on 6 April and ends on the following 5 April. Caused by a historical accident when some days were irretrievably lost.

Tolls – Unexpected taxes, as in: 'it tolls for thee'.

Umbrella – A way of sheltering your unit or investment trusts from bad weather. An umbrella fund has many little funds sheltering beneath it, and you can swap from one to another. Watch out for the ill winds of capital gains tax and stamp duty.

Will – Strong intention to proceed. Where there's a will, there's a way of reducing death duties.

Winding-up – a) Method, such as tax planning, of dealing with the Revenue; b) unfortunate end to a business.

THE AUTHOR

A.J. Carroll hated school. He was hopelessly short-sighted, and thus always last to be picked for team games. Many years later, after university and a spell of teaching, he discovered tax. Finally, he had found a game he could play, enjoy and win.

He has spent fifteen years as a tax adviser, including three in the Far East, a long way offshore. Back home his clients have included a sculptress, an international bank and a breakfast cereal manufacturer. He has now taken shelter with a firm of professional accountants in the City of London.

Along the way he has collected four obscure languages, which comes in useful when translating taxspeak. When he is not dreaming of travel or tax, he writes romantic fiction. He claims this helps him maintain a grasp on reality.